The Good Life

A Guide to Buddhism for the Westerner

By Gerald Roscoe

ASIA BOOKS

Published by Asia Books Company
5 Soi 61 Sukhumvit Road
Bangkok, Thailand
Tel. 391-2680
Fax (662) 381-1621

Produced by Pacific Rim Press
Bangkok, Thailand 1990

Cover Photo by Luca Invernizzi Tettoni

Edited by Dan Reid
Designed by Christopher C. Burt
Typeset by CompuPrint
Printed in Thailand by Darnsutha Press

ISBN #974-8206-56-4 TL-1383

TABLE OF CONTENTS

PREFACE

For several years I have been living in Thailand, where I have been studying and following the path of Buddhism. Thailand is a Buddhist country with a strong monastic community and with a population that is, with the exception of a Muslim minority and an even smaller Christian minority, devoted to the form of Buddhist practice known as *Theravada*.

Theravadans regard their Buddhism as the Way of the Elders, which is the very meaning of Theravada, and is directly derived from the teachings of the Buddha as recorded in the earliest written texts, the *Pali Canon*. *Theravada*, called by some 'The Old Wisdom School' is the Buddhism of southern Asia, Thailand, Burma, Cambodia, and Sri Lanka—whereas *Mahayana*, a later form, is the Buddhism of northern Asia, Tibet, China, Japan (Zen), Mongolia, and Korea.

Buddhism in all its forms is rapidly moving westward, and whether it is practiced in its various permutations—Mahayana, Vajrayana, Zen, Theravada-Tao combined—the permutations are less important than the cohesive core of Buddhism: a belief that the most noble personal pursuit is to follow a path toward enlightenment.

What enlightenment means to a Buddhist and how the Buddhist path is followed are the topics discussed in this book.

Many books have been written about Buddhism, by Edward Conze, Alan Watts, Christmas Humphreys, Alexandra David-Neel, T.W. Rhys-Davids, Kenneth Ch'en, Walpola Rahula, Nancy Wilson Ross, Phra Khantipalo, Huston Smith, John Blofeld, and others. In addition, the Buddhist texts and *suttas* (discourses) have been published in English, though they are not

generally available to the public.

From these sources I have synthesized this concise guide for the Westerner, and to these sources I would refer those who wish to study Buddhism more deeply. But there is yet another source to whom I have turned in the past few years: a German monk at Wat Umong (Suan Buddhadamma) in Chiangmai, Thailand, the Venerable Bhikku Santitittho. At the time of this writing (1989), Phra Santi (as he is best known) had been a Buddhist monk for more than 19 years (he is in his late forties) and had been at Wat Umong for 15 years. He is a man of extraordinary compassion, patience, and Buddhist wisdom, speaks Thai and is as fluent in English as in his native tongue, an exceptional and articulate teacher.

Phra Santi, in the tradition of the Buddha, teaches that Buddhism is non-authoritative, non-ritualistic, non-speculative, non-metaphysical, that it abjures divination, superstition, and soothsaying, that it is empirical, scientific, and pragmatic, that it is psychological, democratic, and, above all, therapeutic. As a Theravadan, Phra Santi teaches that man's enlightenment depends on individual effort rather than on the salvation of others as some Mahayanists believe. This is not to say that it is antisocial; indeed, compassion and fellow-feeling underlie all Buddhist behavior. But enlightenment can only be achieved by one's own diligence. As a Theravadan he believes that there are no superhuman gods or powers, that no one can save us but ourselves. Buddhism is not a matter of faith but rather of seeing, knowing, and understanding the truth which lies hidden within the soul of each individual.

Phra Santi is well-versed in all forms of Buddhism, including Mahayana variants as well as the Theravadan, and he embraces all forms in his ecumenism. He reveres the Bodhisattvas, the saint-like embodiments of Mahayana enlightenment, meditates occasionally with the Tankha paintings of the Tibetan Tantrayana or Vajrayana, and admires Zen Buddhism. All forms, he says, adhere to basic Buddhist concepts but each has developed its own unique form of discipline and instruction. Since different people are at different stages of spiritual development, Buddhism offers different forms from which each person may select the methods best suited for his or her individual requirements.

About six feet tall, heavy-set, weighing some two hundred pounds, Phra Santi has a broad round face, light blue eyes, and a radiant smile. To be in his presence is to feel inspired to emulate his example of serenity, compassion, and wisdom. Every Sunday afternoon at Wat Umong Phra Santi lectures on Buddhism to the many Westerners (and occasional Thais) who gather in a pavilion near his *khuti* (his modest living quarters) to listen to his discourses and to be led by him in a short session of meditation. But every day of the week, sometimes to the detriment of his own solitude and privacy, he greets a steady swarm of visitors to his *khuti*, men and women with questions about Buddhism, with personal problems about which they seek his guidance, or simply with the desire to be in his company. Some visitors even stay for days or weeks in nearby *khutis* specially built by sponsors of Phra Santi to accommodate foreigners. When I once suggested to Phra Santi that perhaps he was too generous with his time, too easily taken advantage of, he replied, with that wonderful smile, "It is my responsibility and my joy to be helpful."

I hope that in his having assisted me so notably in the preparation of this book he will derive some satisfaction in knowing that I listened well to his words.

CHAPTER ONE: THE APPEAL OF BUDDHISM

More than five hundred years older than Christianity, one of the great, enduring religions of Eastern civilization, Buddhism is today finding new sources of strength and vitality in the Western world.

Increasingly, throughout Europe, Great Britain, America, and elsewhere, men and women in search of meaningful lives are being attracted to Buddhism, often motivated at first by intellectual curiosity and then finding a deeply gratifying spiritual nourishment.

As the French expression puts it, "Je suis atheiste...mais Catholique", so it may be said by many Western practitioners, "I am Christian...but Buddhist", or "I am Jewish...but Buddhist". It certainly may be said, "I am atheist...but Buddhist", for Buddhism does not worship a God but concerns itself with more human, immediate, and practical matters than whether there is a God. It's worth noting that an acceptance of Buddhism does not necessarily require a rejection of one's parental or earlier-life religion. A Buddhist is respectful of all religions.

In fact, Buddhism does not *require* anything of those who would practice it—for Buddhism is not dogmatic nor catechistic. It does not preach sin. It does not say there is only one right way. It merely offers a path to wisdom, to enlightenment; the very word Buddha is derived from *buddh*, to be 'awake', to be 'enlightened'. The Buddha was a human being, not a divinity, a fully enlightened human being who was above all a teacher.

What the Buddha taught was how to live the 'good life'. This is what he taught both the monk and the layperson. For both, living a good life leads, the Buddha taught, to *nirvana*, a concept quite difficult for the Western mind to grasp. In the case of a monk, *nirvana* is less difficult to attain than in the case of a layperson, because the renunciate, devoted, meditating monk follows 227(!) precepts of behavior and can thus more easily overcome whatever deficiencies there may have been in the *karma* inherited from previous lives—another difficult concept for the Western mind—or whatever bad *karma* he may have accumulated in the years prior to his donning the robes of the monkhood.

For the moment, rather than attempting to explain the various esoteric dimensions of *karma*, a simple but nonetheless accurate definition is that "good deeds have good effects, bad deeds have bad effects". To a Buddhist the bad deeds he or she may have committed in previous lives are obstacles to spiritual fulfillment, or to the attainment of *nirvana*, in this life. But this life gives one an opportunity to clean the slate, so to speak, by an accumulation of good deeds, of good *karma*.

Even if a Westerner has difficulty accepting the notion of past and future lives, the individual with a sense of morality (which may be said of all human beings, even those whose behavior is at times immoral) does accept that doing good is better than doing evil. It's better for one's conscience, better for one's peace of mind, better for one's spiritual serenity. Never mind a future life, never mind *nirvana*. In this life, here and now, merit and a good conscience bring their own rewards.

So for the layman as well as the monk, Buddhism offers a way of life which in many ways is similar to that offered by Christianity, Judaism, Hinduism, Islam, or any of the world's religions.

The similarities between Buddhism and other religions lie in their approach to morality: the Christian-Judaic commandments; the Islamic code; the Buddhist precepts.

The Buddhist layperson, unlike the Buddhist monk, pledges to undertake the rules of training by observing five precepts: to (1) refrain from destroying life, (2) from taking what is not given, (3) from illicit sexual relationships, (4) from false speech, and (5) from intoxicants causing heedlessness. These precepts are discussed in subsequent chapters.

Note that the preface to the Five Precepts contains the words, "I undertake the rule of training to refrain from...", an assertion of individual responsibility quite different from the divine *commandments* of the Hebraic and Christian decalogue.

The major dissimilarity between Buddhism and the other religions lies in the Buddhist perception of *dukkha*. In Buddhism there is no more important word, no more important concept than that of *dukkha*. (In any discussion of Theravada Buddhism it is difficult, and inadvisable, to avoid Pali words like *dukkha* because there are simply no adequate English equivalents. Pali is the ancient language in which Theravada Buddhist teachings have been preserved, while Sanskrit is the ancient language of Mahayana Buddhism). The Pali word, *dukkha* is often translated, rather inadequately, as suffering or pain, but it has connotations far beyond that meaning. In Pali the word was also used for an off-center axle or for a dislocated bone, a connotation useful to remember when coming across *dukkha* in Buddhist teachings.

The experiences which the Buddha listed as examples of *dukkha* serve more satisfactorily than any attempt at definition. What the Buddha taught was:

Birth is *dukkha*, a shocking, traumatic experience.

Sickness is *dukkha*, with its pains, its fevers, its discomforts, its anguish.

Decay, decrepitude, and old age are *dukkha*, with strength and vigor diminishing, with appetites waning, with vital organs faltering, with dependence on others increasing.

Death is *dukkha*, as is the fear of death.

To have to endure what one dislikes is *dukkha*.

To be separated from what one likes or from the people one loves is *dukkha*.

Attachment to what Buddhism calls the five *khandhas*, the five aggregates which make up an individual body, feelings, perceptions, intentions and acts of consciousness, is *dukkha*.

Attachment to the notion of a 'self' apart from the five *khandhas*, a controlling, permanent, perhaps immortal unity considered to be 'self', is *dukkha*.

So, whether *dukkha* is described as that which is suffering, painful, unsatisfactory, diseased, dislocated, unendurable or abhorrent, what the man born as Siddartha Gotama saw before he became the Buddha was that the cycle of human life is inescapably *dukkha*. What he set out to find was a way for people to put an end to their *dukkha*, and it was this that he found when he became enlightened at the age of 35 and devoted the remaining 45 years of his life to teaching. As he himself put it: "What I teach is *dukkha* and the cessation of *dukkha*."

The teachings of the Buddha are essentially based on the Four Noble Truths of Buddhism, the first of which is: There is *dukkha*. It should be noted, however, that the Buddhist acceptance of *dukkha* does not imply denial of the existence of happiness, joy, achievement, fulfillment, of the ease and well-being that are described in the Pali word *sukkha*, the antithesis of *dukkha*.

The Buddhist does, nonetheless, believe that the most overwhelming characteristic of existence is *dukkha*, especially if one lacks the wisdom to know life as it really is.

What appeals particularly to Western Buddhists who accept and understand the First Noble Truth, the concept of *dukkha*, is the teaching of the Buddha's Fourth Noble Truth; that *dukkha* can be eliminated by following what he called the Noble Eightfold Path.

I am postponing discussion of the Second Noble Truth, that the cause of dukkha is craving, and the Third Noble Truth, that the elimination of craving brings about enlightenment, or *nirvana*, in order to concentrate first on the Fourth Noble Truth and the Noble Eightfold Path.

The Buddha teaches eight activities in his Noble Path, contained in three groupings: those required for the cultivation of ethical conduct, those required for the cultivation of mental discipline, and those required for the cultivation of insight-wisdom. The moral and the mental cultivations are what most Western Buddhists find especially rewarding, perhaps because they are the easiest to comprehend and accept, and it is with these that they usually begin their practice of Buddhism and embark on the Path. The insight-wisdom teachings are regarded by many as being beyond the understanding of all but the most advanced of practicing Buddhist laypersons—Asian as well as Western and possibly even beyond the understanding of most monks, except for a handful of devoted renunciates and the elders of the Buddhist monastic order. However, they are not so arcane or esoteric as to be totally incomprehensible. Intense practice of the Noble Path leads directly to comprehension of the Buddha's teachings. We'll come to them further on, after we consider the ethical-conduct and mental-discipline cultivations taught by the Buddha.

But first let's have a brief look at the Buddha and his life.

TWO: THE BUDDHA

One of the glories of mankind is the appearance on earth of the truly unique, truly great individual, the genius who influences the world.

There are many shining examples of such individuals, rare though they may be among the billions who have inhabited the earth. To take some examples, in literature there is Shakespeare; in music Mozart, in art Leonardo, in philosophy Plato, in science Einstein, in religion Jesus and Moses and Muhammad and Confucius—and a man named Siddartha Gotama, the man who became the Buddha.

Siddartha Gotama was a both a real historical character and a mythical man of legend.

Born around 560 B.C. in a prosperous kingdom of northern India, now Nepal, he was the son of a king and heir to the throne. He lived his early life as a prince, protected by his parents from the harsh realities of life in the outside world and grew up in luxury. He was a man of exceptional physical appearance—there are numerous references to the perfection of his physical body. He married a beautiful young woman, sired a handsome son, and was destined to inherit his father's position of wealth, power, and prestige.

But in his twenties he renounced his royal inheritance, his temporal fortunes, and even his family, after having witnessed what legend calls the Four Passing Sights. One day, on seeing a decrepit old man he became aware of old age. Another day he saw a diseased person lying on the road and became aware of illness. On a third day he saw a corpse and became aware of death. These sights filled him with despair, but on a fourth day he saw a Brahman monk, and in thinking about the life of a renunciate he decided that he too would renounce his worldly estate and go forth to seek an understanding of what made life so full of what he later described as *dukkha*, and to seek the truth of existence leading to the cessation of *dukkha*.

He was twenty-nine when he made the break. For six years he lived as a solitary forest-dweller, at first as the disciple of two renowned Hindu masters. Then, after deciding he had learned all they could teach him—which he felt was not enough—he joined a band of ascetics and with them he practiced such extreme austerities and ate so little that he nearly died. Study with the Hindus had not brought him the enlightenment he was seeking, nor had his experiment with asceticism. Rejecting self-indulgence as well as self-mortification, he determined to follow what he called the Middle Path and to devote himself to a course of mental cultivation and mystical concentration.

In the town of Bodhgaya in northeast India, Siddartha Gotama sat down beneath a fig tree (the Bo tree, from *Bodhi*, enlightenment) to embark on an extended period of meditation, and determined not to rise until he had found the truth. For forty-nine days he meditated, formulating a body of wisdom which was to bring mankind a new religion. When he arose he was enlightened, he was a Buddha, ready to go forth and teach others how to become enlightened.

Soon after his enlightenment the Buddha preached to a small group of the curious and those who heard his words became his disciples. From then on the Buddha devoted the rest of his life to teaching those who sought his advice, his compassion, his wisdom. The growth in the number of his disciples led to his establishment of the *Sangha*, the Buddhist monastic order, and it was his disciples who passed along his teachings, by word of mouth, from generation to generation. Not until some considerable time after his *parinirvana*, or his death, were the words of the Buddha recorded in written form.

As with other historic religious leaders, a vast literature of wonderful and beautiful legend about the Buddha was to be written by his followers, but the realities of Siddartha Gotama's life and his realization of enlightenment are as I have briefly summarized them.

The rapid spread of Buddhism through Asia, and now through the Western world, is beyond the intention and scope of this concise work, but suffice it to say that Siddartha Gotama, the Buddha, changed the world, and that his message, his wisdom and his teachings have been received with appreciation and reverence by millions of individuals searching for the good life.

"Look within", the Buddha taught, "for thou art Buddha."

THREE: THE CULTIVATION OF ETHICAL CONDUCT

How does one become a Buddhist?

There are no formal inductions, no initiations, no baptisms. I once asked an English artist how he had become a Buddhist. His answer was, "I didn't become a Buddhist. I realized that I am a Buddhist." Most Western Buddhists will agree with him.

The realization that one is a Buddhist may be formally confirmed by repeating three times, "To the Buddha I go for refuge; to the Dhamma (the teachings of Buddhism) I go for refuge; to the Sangha (the Buddhist monastic community) I go for refuge." For those who have access to a Buddhist temple (or monk) these words, of refuge in the Triple Gem, are spoken in the presence of a monk, and are followed by saying aloud the Five Precepts.

The Westerner who regards himself or herself as a Buddhist is making a profound personal and social statement. That person is saying, on setting out to follow the Path: I believe, as the Buddha taught, that I should conduct myself with benevolence, compassion, joyous sympathy, and equanimity. I believe that these qualities are the basis of ethical conduct and that ethical conduct should be the basis of society.

The Buddha's prescriptions for the cultivation of ethical conduct—namely, **Right Action, Right Speech, and Right Livelihood** derive from his conception of society based on universal love and compassion.

Right Action promotes honorable and peaceful conduct and is based on the five precepts: abstention from destroying life, from stealing, from illicit sex, from intoxicants, from falsehoods.

In *abstaining from destroying life*, some Buddhists, lay and monastic, will not kill insects or eat the flesh of animals, and there are even some monks who will not destroy plant life, will not cut down a tree or a bush, will not pull out a blade of grass, will not drink water without first having filtered it to prevent the destruction of whatever living beings might be in the water.

In *abstaining from stealing*, there is the explicit admonition not to take that which is not offered. This is particularly applicable to monks who as mendicants do not reach out for the food or alms presented to them but instead wait until such offerings are placed in their hands, their alms-bowls, or at their fingertips.

In *abstaining from illicit sex*, there are explicit proscriptions against adulterous sex, sex with minors, sex with those who are celibate. The Buddha also advised sexual restraint and moderation for the lay person (total abstinence, of course, for the monk).

In *abstaining from intoxicants*, the precept literally says "...distilled and fermented intoxicants producing heedlessness." (I once asked the abbot of a temple in Bangkok why so many Thais, presumably good Buddhists, consumed alcohol. He said he could condone it as long as they did not become "heedless" a most liberal interpretation of the precept, but not strictly in adherence to the teachings.)

In *abstaining from false speech*, the precept is intended to abjure more improprieties than just lying. False Speech is the opposite of:

Right Speech An amplification of the precept on falsehood, 'Right Speech' (which, of course, derives from right thought) promotes courteous, considerate, non-contentious conduct. It requires abstention from harsh language, from slander, from gossip, from bearing false witness.

Right Livelihood promotes life instead of destroying life. It requires abstention from earning a living in any way that harms others: slaughter of animals, trading in arms, drugs, intoxicants, living beings, or poisons.

The Buddha said: Your means of livelihood should be honorable, blameless, and innocent of harm to others.

(There are some who feel that if the Buddha were living today he might modify what he said about Right Livelihood, since the slaughter of animals for food, and the trading of arms for a nation's security are social necessities. Perhaps. The slaughter of animals is the destruction of life, but there are those who rationalize it as being permissible in order to provide human food needs. The trading of arms leads to the destruction of life, but some rationalize that it is permissible in the defense of a nation and its people. I leave it to the brewers, vintners, and distillers to rationalize their own defense.)

Right Action, Right Speech, and Right Livelihood lie at the core of Buddhist ethical conduct. They influence all aspects of behavior: personal behavior, family behavior, social behavior. In various discourses (*suttas* in Pali, *sutras* in Sanskrit) the Buddha offered specific and detailed instructions for laypersons regarding virtually every aspect of moral behavior in everyday life (Chapter 7). Moral behavior, the Buddha taught, was the first and indispensable step in following the Path. Without moral behavior it would be difficult, indeed impossible, to succeed in mental cultivation and insight-wisdom.

FOUR: MENTAL CULTIVATION

The second major aspect of Buddhism that attracts many Westerners is the one which deals with mental cultivation, especially as it pertains to meditation. The significance of meditation in what the Buddha taught is underscored by his having devoted to it three of the eight steps in the Noble Path: **Right Effort, Right Mindfulness,** and **Right Concentration.**

Right Effort lies in developing the will power to change our habits of thought; and in developing the insight and intuition to perceive our states of mind. The Buddha stressed the need, if one would follow the path successfully, to make a strenuous effort. Man's difficulties derive from ignorance, he said, not sin, and can be confronted and overcome through techniques that can be taught if one makes the right effort to learn. It is not easy to develop virtues, to curb passions, to overcome deluded states of mind. Effective mind cultivation takes effort, commitment and persistent meditation.

Right Mindfulness requires unremitting awareness applied to every thought, every word, every deed in order to keep one's mind in control of one's senses. (There is a form of meditation, *Vipassana*, that specifically nurtures mindfulness, discussed below.)

Right Concentration is, in short, right meditation for calming the mind.

MEDITATION

There exist today, and have existed in the past, many different forms of meditation, among which are those practiced by the Christian monks of the Egyptian desert, by the Jains, the

Sufis, the Hindu Yogins, Catholic monastics, Transcendental Meditators, Tantric Tibetans, Zen disciples, etc. What concerns us here because of their growing appeal to contemporary Westerners are the forms of meditation practiced by Theravada Buddhists.

Nancy Wilson Ross in her lucid *Buddhism, A Way of Life and Thought* gives us these illuminating words, which serve as a helpful preface to an understanding of the practice of Buddhist meditation:

"Man (sets out) in single-hearted pursuit of satisfaction as if it actually represented a constant. Yet, in the Buddha's view, it was this very belief in the attainment of lasting happiness, in conventional human terms, that was the true source of suffering (*dukkha*). Man, by his unwillingness to accept what he interprets as life's failures to give him without stint whatever he desires, finds himself caught in an emotional trap of his own making. This trap is the product of his (belief in his) ego. It takes form from the self's insatiable appetites and delusions, its enormous blind unattainable desires, its never-satisfied craving or thirst (for which the Buddhist Pali word is *tanha*). It is *tanha* which leads the individual to place a tacit demand on life which life by its very nature cannot fulfill.

"How then can a man find peace in the midst of continuous blind striving and impermanence? There is only one way, and that way must teach the development of compassionate detachment and discernment: an ever-deepening awareness of the interdependence and relationship of the individual with the cosmos. As for a definite path to the development of such awareness, with its resultant dynamic tranquility, there is only one hope: *directed meditation or constant mindfulness.*"

The type of meditation which most Western Buddhist laypersons practice is *Samatha*, the development of calm and concentration to focus and quiet the mind. *Samatha* has been likened to a cooling of the mind (and the body), and is being prescribed more and more frequently in the Western world by physicians in the treatment of hypertension and other cardiovascular disorders. (Cf. *The Relaxation Response* by Dr. Robert Lindner, Harvard Medical School.) Indeed, those who practice *Samatha* meditation have learned that it brings them welcome serenity in a world of frenzy. The Buddha perceived this stilling of mind, this serenity, as a means to balanced behavior.

(I once brought a friend of mine, a high-powered businessman, to visit Phra Santi at Wat Umong, and my friend said that his life was too frenetic for him to sit down daily and meditate. Phra Santi patiently explained to him that is precisely why he should, and taught him in only a few minutes the breathing-in, breathing-out form of meditation. Later my friend told me it had changed his life.)

Stilling the mind is not easily accomplished. No greater evidence of the impermanence of things, as taught by the Buddha, may be found than in the workings of the mind. Only in the most intense kinds of concentration—creative, scientific, and communicative—can the mind be focussed to remain more than a few seconds on any one given subject. Ordinarily, as Buddhists say, the mind jumps unceasingly and restlessly like a monkey in a cage. The mind flitters hither and thither like a butterfly. As unrestrained and untamed as our dreams are, no less so is our mental stream of consciousness when we are awake. In fact, psychologists have learned that we cannot sustain a random thought sequence for more than three and a half seconds. The kinetic, electromagnetic, energy of the mind has a life of its own. The goal of *Samatha* meditation is to slow down the mental activities, to control the mental wanderings, to *ignore* sensory reactions of sight, sound, smell, taste, touch, to *ignore* the kinetics of the mind.

There are several forms of *Samatha* meditation. The Buddha recommended specific forms for specific types of personality—the greedy person, the angry person, the intelligent person, and so on—and he even taught how the different types of personality reveal themselves and can be identified. But the one form of *Samatha* he recommended to all persons was the breathing-in, breathing-out meditation.

This form of meditation is simple to do and simple to describe. Sit on the floor, a shallow cushion is permitted in the half-lotus position, the legs crossed at the knees with the right leg lying on the left. (The full lotus position is too difficult for most Westerners to sustain.) Hold your spine erect, hands in your lap with palms upward, left hand under right, thumbs touching at their tips, eyes closed, chin in. Make yourself comfortable in this position. (You may, also, meditate while sitting erect on a hard chair, maintaining the same upper body posture.)

Concentrate on the passage of breath in and out through your nostrils, or the rising and falling of the abdomen.

That's all there is to it.

Try not to let sounds, smells, sights, touch, tastes or mental activities distract you from the one thing you're doing: observing your breathing in and breathing out. Do this for at least ten minutes, try to go twenty minutes, even longer. Do it every day, morning or evening, or both.

Now, although I've described it as simple to do, it's not simple to do effectively. The mind is not easily stilled. So, don't be impatient when your mind jumps, as it will. In the middle of an in-breath your mind will jump to a business problem, a family problem, a sensual thought, a pleasant memory, a distasteful one. You'll hear a door being slammed, an airplane overhead, a baby crying, a radio playing, a horn honking. You'll feel an itch on your scalp, a twitch in a leg muscle, a stirring in your digestive system. Just try to ignore these distractions and get back to your concentration on breathing in and breathing out. At first you'll find it difficult and you may be discouraged. In time, as you practice meditation, you'll be able to ignore distractions for a few seconds, even a few minutes. You will not be able to ignore them for the entire time of your meditation. But no matter. Even a brief stilling of the mind is beneficial. (Some meditators, monks especially, do succeed in stilling the mind for long enough periods of time to enter trance-like states of concentration—called *jhanas*—in which there is one-pointedness of mind and there are no distractions affecting the mind, no sensations other than happiness, joy, insight.)

The Buddha said: "the mind is flighty, difficult to subdue, flitting wherever it chooses. To tame the mind is good. A mind tamed can bring happiness."

For many Western meditators the beneficial effects of *Samatha* are sufficient rewards for their effort: calm, serenity, tranquility, lessening of tensions. But there are, of course, other effects which the consistent meditator ultimately perceives: the realization that the self is not the master of sensory perceptions or mental activities; the recognition of impermanence and constant change; in short, the awareness that is the goal of the other major form of meditation known as *Vipassana*.

(I was first introduced to meditation by the abbot of Wat Saket in Bangkok and by one of the senior monks who was a meditation master. After a few weeks of practice I asked them what I was supposed to get out of it and what my goals in meditation should be. I was told; don't ask, just do. I found that answer not very helpful, and I regret that I was not told that my meditations were intended to still my mind and to induce awareness.

Had I been told, my meditation practice would have been more effective more quickly. But I also understand, now, that the good abbot and his meditation master were not being flippant or unresponsive in their "don't ask, just do." For some people—and this is what Zen masters believe—just doing leads to an understanding of why they are meditating. For me it did not. I mention this because many of my Western friends, like me at first, become discouraged if they "just do" without understanding why.

(I might add that I have found a technique that may be helpful to start-up meditators. While on one mental level I am concentrating on "observing" my breath, on another level I am picturing my mind being cooled by a gentle flow of water. Or picturing the illumination of my brain being slowly turned down as if by a rheostat. Or picturing the flames of my mind, as on a gas range, being adjusted lower and lower, until only the pilot light still burns softly.

(Phra Santi recommends similar images, as well as the silent wording of *Bud*—on each in-breath,—*dho* on each out-breath. He also recommends thinking, and concentrating on, "Here...Now. Now...Here.")

A second method of *Samatha* cultivation is the walking meditation, very popular in the East, less so in the West. In one of its forms, the meditator walks slowly back and forth, in a natural, harmonious pace, hands held loosely in front of the body or in back, eyes lowered to a spot six feet or so in advance of one's walking. In another form, one concentrates on the movements and actions of walking: I am raising my left foot, I am moving it forward, I am putting it down. I am raising my right foot, I am moving it forward, I am putting it down. I am stopping. I am turning. I am moving forward again. I am raising my left foot. And so on.

By concentrating so intently on walking, one finds it easy—easier than in breathing meditation—to ignore distractions. No question that it is a beneficial one-mindedness exercise. Whether it is as tranquilizing an exercise as breathing meditation is questionable.

A third form of *Samatha* is that practiced in Transcendental Meditation, as well as in Tibetan and other meditative practices: recitation of sacred syllables, or *mantras*. One such sacred syllable is the Brahmanic *Aum*—in Buddhism *Om*—the syllable believed to be the first primordial sound. In Hindu belief the creative power in *Aum* helped bring forth the world and represents all aspects of the universe.

In the well-known mantra *Om Mani Padme Hum*, as explained by John Blofeld in *The Tantric Mysteries of Tibet*, *Om* stands for the totality of sound, the totality of existence; *Mani* for the highest value within our own mind, "the pure void which is always to be found there when the intervening layers of murky consciousness are pierced"; *Padme*, which means lotus, for the spiritual unfolding leading to *Mani*; *Hum* for our potential enlightenment.

(I have occasionally heard Phra Santi chant *Om Mani Padme Hum*, the *Om* starting deep and soft in his throat, echoing in his mouth, rising to his nasal passages, emerging vibratory from his lips—an experience verging on the mystical and one which could convince even the cynical of the efficacy of chanting when done as it was intended to be done.)

Yet another form of *Samatha* meditation recommended by Theravadan Buddhists for developing calm and concentration to focus and quiet the mind is *Kasina*. One fixes one's attention on a colored disc, and then with eyes closed recalls the image. The various forms of colored discs and backgrounds which one constructs oneself are earth symbols, aids to one-mindedness and tranquility. *Kasina* is, however, not a widely practiced form of meditation.

Vipassana meditation, as contrasted with *Samatha*, is the specific mental cultivation of awareness. Whereas in *Samatha* one ignores sensory, mental, and physical actions and diversions, in *Vipassana* one intentionally notices them. It is an intense and demanding meditation. For minutes, hours, even days, the meditator concentrates on noticing every action, every thought, every feeling. When eating, for example, one is aware of the fork rising, coming to the mouth, of the food in the mouth, of the food being chewed, being swallowed, of the fork moving away, of the fork being put down. And so with everything one does or thinks, one strives to be aware of what is happening in the most minute detail.

The goal of *Vipassana* is the realization that the five *khandhas*—body, feelings, perceptions, intentions and volitions (mental formations), and acts of consciousness—are constantly taking place independently of the self; that there is no self at their controls. Such awareness frees one from the attachment to self, because it reveals the ever-changing, impermanent nature of the *khandhas*, the aggregates of existence, (*dukkha* if one is ignorant of their true nature). This freeing from self helps one cultivate insight-wisdom, helps one become gradually more intelligent about the true nature of life while pursuing the path to its ultimate goal, enlightenment.

Other forms of meditation, although not generally practiced by laypersons, and only infrequently by monks, are those intended primarily for the cultivation of character, rather than for the cultivation of tranquility, one-mindedness, or insight. These consist of meditations on the qualities of the Buddha, on his teachings, and on the monastic order, intended to induce better understanding of the Triple Gem; meditation on the composition of the body, its unattractive components, sinews, blood, bones, acids, fluids, etc., intended to induce a lessening of attachment to the total physical self; meditation on death, intended to stimulate energy here and now, as well as preparation for and fearlessness of the inevitable; and meditation on universal love, *metta*. Further discussion of these interesting and worthwhile meditations, however, lies beyond the intentions of this concise guide. The interested reader is referred to the many fine books that have been written specifically on the subject of meditation.

FIVE: INSIGHT-WISDOM CULTIVATION

The whole range of Buddhist discipline and Buddhist teaching culminates in the cultivation of insight-wisdom. In the Buddha's view the cultivation of ethical conduct is the first requirement for the development of discipline, the indispensable foundation on which to build the cultivation of mental tranquility, one-mindedness, and awareness required for meditation. Meditation is the basis on which insight-wisdom is built, insight into things as they really are.

In order to attain insight-wisdom one must have the **Right View**, the view that there are three fundamental truths: one, all existence—if an individual is ignorant of the true nature of things—is suffering (as covered by *dukkha*, which has been reviewed above); two, all existence is transitory or impermanent; and three, there is no permanent self or soul.

In order to energize **Right View** one should cultivate **Right Thought**, which means right motivation and right attitude. This involves freeing oneself from what the Buddha called the three major defilements: **greed, anger, and delusion.**

Anger needs no further definition.

Greed is defined in the Buddhist concept (*tanha*) as craving, egoistic desire, attachment. The Second Noble Truth, deferred until now, is that the cause of suffering (*dukkha*) is *tanha*, in all its meanings. The Third Noble Truth is that the elimination of *tanha* brings about the cessation of suffering.

Delusion, also known as 'ignorance', is the absence of insight-wisdom, the lack of understanding of the Four Noble Truths: There is suffering; the cause of suffering is egoistic desire;

the elimination of egoistic desire eliminates suffering; the way to the elimination of egoistic desire is the Noble Eightfold Path.

Many Western Buddhists stop short of the cultivation of insight-wisdom, restricting their practice to the cultivation of ethical conduct and the cultivation of mental development through meditation. Those who stop short may do so out of fear that the Buddha's teachings on insight-wisdom are too esoteric, too complicated to comprehend and too demanding to be absorbed into their practical day-to-day lives. They may not have the benefit of access to articulate teachers (like Phra Santi) or to simplified written elucidations. Unfortunately, much of what has been written about Buddhist insight-wisdom, especially by Asian writers, is incomprehensibly abstract, owing in large part to the different ways in which Asians understand such Buddhist concepts as *dukkha*, suffering, of *tanha*, craving, of *anicca*, impermanence, of *anatta*, no-self, of *karma*, cause-and-effect, of rebirth, of *nirvana*. Asian writers understand and appreciate the connotations of the Pali (or Sanskrit) terms without, often, defining them adequately for the Western reader.

Dukkha has already been reviewed.

Tanha should be understood as craving, egoistic (and sensual) desire, attachment. As the Buddha viewed it, sensual craving, craving for eternal existence, craving for perpetual youth, for constant good health, for temporal happiness, and so on, are the sources of *dukkha*, of man's disease, anguish, suffering, and unhappiness. Craving may lead to doing harm to others. It may lead to inner anxieties and tensions brought on by the struggle to attain what is craved, the fear of not succeeding in the attainment, or the fear of losing what has been attained. Craving ensnares us. The pleasures derived from sensual craving, craving for eternal existence, and craving for temporal happiness cannot satisfy our most heart-felt longings.

We crave, Buddhism teaches, because we are attached to the notion of 'self', from which we can release ourselves by conscious and strenuous effort at detachment. And detachment is a consequence of the cultivation of insight-wisdom. When we detach from craving, we detach from suffering.

Anicca, impermanence, is defined by Christmas Humphreys in *A Popular Dictionary of Buddhism* as: "One of the three characteristics of all existence; the others being *Dukkha* and *Anatta*. Buddhism teaches that everything is subject to the law of cause and effect, is the creation of preceding causes and is in turn a cause of after-effects. There is in existence, therefore, no unchanging condition of being, but only an ever-becoming flux."

Although impermanence—constant flux—is an absolute characteristic of all existence, there are those who are unable to recognize or unwilling to accept its reality, and these are the people who, in their delusion, the Buddha said, create for themselves a false belief in a permanent 'self'. Most people, however, accept the notion of impermanence, even though they have difficulty with the notion of 'no-self'. Insight-wisdom helps one come to grips with both notions.

Anatta, 'no-self'. In *Buddhism, the Light of Asia*, Kenneth Ch'en gives us these very helpful observations: "The Buddha held that belief in a permanent self or soul is one of the most deceitful delusions ever held by man, for it gives rise to attachment, attachment to egoism, egoism to cravings for pleasure and fame, which in turn lead to suffering. He held that this false belief in a permanent self is due to an erroneous conception of a unity behind the elements that combine to make up an individual.

"He said that he had searched everywhere for this permanent self or soul, (this unity), but found only a conglomeration of the five *khandhas* or aggregates—material body, feelings, perception, predispositions (intentions and volitions, mental formations), and consciousness. At any one moment, according to him, we are but a temporary composition of the five aggregates, and as these change every moment, so does the composition. Therefore all that we are is but a continuous living entity which does not remain the same for any two consecutive moments, but which comes into being and disappears as soon as it arises.

"Why then should we attach so much importance to this transitory entity, in which there is no permanent self or soul? Once we accept this truth of the non-existence of a permanent self, when we see that what we call the self is nothing but a stream of perishing physical and psychical phenomena, then we destroy our selfish desires and self-interests, and instead of suffering from anxieties and disappointments, we will enjoy peace of mind and tranquility." This is another truth revealed by the cultivation of insight-wisdom.

One should not think *I* am in pain, but rather there is pain; not that *I* am angry but rather there is anger; not that *I* am joyful but rather there is joy. In short, not "*I* am" but rather "there is". One should realize that whatever arises, i.e. whatever "there is" such as pain, feelings, sensations, thoughts, emotions soon passes away. It is the law of impermanence: what arises passes away. Thus, one should realize that *I*, although a useful and necessary social-communicative term, cannot be regarded as a permanent self. It should not, and cannot, be clung to.

Most Western Buddhists I have known are intellectually oriented academics, professionals, writers, artists, and the like. For them there is this paradox: although they can accept, with their minds, what the Buddha said about 'no-self', it is difficult for them to accept, with their hearts that they have no 'self' with which to control their intellect and, indeed, their emotions. The Westerner, especially the intellectual, is inclined to believe that he or she is 'in control' and 'in charge' of his or her life.

Buddhism does not gainsay this. Although there is no self, no soul, Buddhism says, as Kenneth Ch'en further explains that, "...there is only a living complex of mental and physical elements succeeding one another continuously, living on the fruits of its acts. Because of this it can control itself and can exert efforts to better itself, so that by the proper discipline it is able to attain *nirvana* or deliverance." (Or—short of nirvana—and in terms more immediately relevant for a practical Westerner—to teach at a university, or to write a novel, or to design a building, or to succeed at any kind of sustained effort in the arts, in science, in the professions, in business.) Yes, there is that which controls: *karma*, not self.

With *karma* we come to another of the difficult and frequently misunderstood Buddhist concepts. Here is one of the better explanations, as provided by Huston Smith in *The Religions of Man*:

"(1) There is a thread of causation threading each life to those which have led up to it and those which will follow. That is to say, each life is in the condition it is in because of the way the lives which have led into it were lived.

"(2) In the midst of this causal sequence, man's will remains free. Though the orderliness of the world sees to it that up to a point acts will be followed by predictable consequences, these consequences never shackle man's will or determine completely what he must do. Man remains a free agent, always at liberty to do something to effect his destiny.

"(3) Though these points assume the importance of causal connections in life, none of them requires the notion of a lump of mental substance (a 'self') that is passed on from life to life.

Impressions, ideas, feelings, 'streams of consciousness', 'present moments' (volitional activities, as will be further explained by Walpola Rahula, below)—these are all that we find, no underlying spiritual substrata...if there be an enduring self, subject always, never object, it cannot be found."

For an understanding of other important dimensions of *karma* we turn to the scholarly Sri Lankan monk Walpola Rahula and his *What the Buddha Taught*:

"The Buddha's own definition of *karma* should be remembered: 'It is volition that I call *karma*. Having willed, one acts through body, speech, and mind.' Volition is 'mental construction, mental activity. Its function is to direct the mind in the sphere of good, bad, or neutral activities.'

"It is only volitional actions—such as intention, will, determination, confidence, concentration, wisdom, energy, desire, repugnance or hate, ignorance, conceit, idea of self, etc.—that can produce karmic effects."

These volitional activities are included in the aggregate, the *khandha*, of mental formations (and are mistaken for self).

Walpola Rahula also writes: "The theory of *karma* should not be confused with so-called 'moral justice' or 'reward and punishment'. (These ideas) arise out of the conception of a supreme being, a God, who sits in judgment, who is a law-giver and who decides what is right and wrong. The theory of *karma* is the theory of cause and effect, of action and reaction; it is a natural law, which has nothing to do with the idea of justice or reward or punishment. Every volitional action produces its effects or results. If a good action produces good effects and a bad action bad effects...this is in virtue of its own nature, its own law."

An understanding of *karma* brings with it a better appreciation of the Buddhist views on rebirth. Walpola Rahula's comments are especially helpful:

"What is difficult (to understand) is that, according to the *karma* theory, the effects of a volitional action may continue to manifest themselves even in a life after death. Here we have to explain what death is according to Buddhism.

"We have seen earlier that a being is nothing but a combination of physical and mental forces or energies. What we call death is the total non-functioning of the physical body. Do all these forces and energies stop with the non-functioning of the body? Buddhism says, no. Will, volition, desire, thirst to exist, to continue to become more and more, is a tremendous force that moves whole lives, whole existences, that even moves the whole world. This is the greatest force, the greatest energy in the world. According to Buddhism, this force does not stop with the non-functioning of the body, which is death; but it continues manifesting itself in another form, producing re-existence which is called rebirth."

One may ask, if there is rebirth, why can I not recall previous lives? The Buddhist answer is that you cannot because your powers of memory are not strong enough. One form of Buddhist meditation dramatizes this inability to remember. It calls for the meditator to recall the activities of the previous day—every one of the activities—in reverse chronological order from the moment of retiring back to the moment of arising. Then try to recall the activities of the day before, and so on. Very difficult.

Nonetheless, you and I can recall certain events from our past, even from early childhood, but we cannot—because of its trauma—recall birth. Nor what preceded it in previous lives. There are some who claim they can, and perhaps they are right. In

Tibetan Buddhism they seem quite surely to be right, as is evidenced by the rigid techniques by which future Dalai Lamas are required in childhood to recall and identify things possessed in a former life. The Buddha himself said that consistent meditation could bring one a recall of former lives, and it is believed that some monks have developed the ability to recall.

(I once asked the 90-year old abbot of a Buddhist temple in Sankhampaeng, near Chiangmai, if he had this ability. He replied that this was a question no monk was allowed by the rules of the monastic order, the *Sangha*, to answer, because to answer 'yes' would be boastful whereas to answer 'no' might be untruthfull. A monk should not make any claim to spiritual attainment, powers, or degrees of enlightenment. And yet I took for an answer a twinkle in the eyes of this gentle abbot as he smiled down at me from his elevated platform.)

According to Buddhist belief, the karmic force of one's rebirth may manifest itself in many diverse forms—insects, animals, incorporeal gods and tormented spirits, as well, of course, human beings, which is the most desirable form of rebirth. For only a human being has the opportunity to cultivate one's moral conduct and mental discipline and insight-wisdom—one's *karma*—in order to put an end to the cycle of rebirth and achieve *nirvana.*

Nirvana is interpreted by Buddhists on two levels. Classical Buddhists claim *nirvana* is attained, at the end of one's life, only when the ultimate goal of the Buddhist is realized: the ending of the cycle of rebirth. According to contemporary Buddhists, *nirvana* not only has this interpretation but is also seen as enlightenment attainable during one's lifetime. In either case *nirvana* is the culmination of having successfully followed the Noble Eightfold Path; of having realized the realities of *dukkha*, impermanence, and 'no-self'; of having liberated oneself from craving, anger and delusion; of having lived morally, meditatively, and with insight-wisdom.

One who has achieved *nirvana*, who is truly enlightened, will not be reborn, will have escaped the continuity of *dukkha*. This definitely does not mean to a Buddhist that *nirvana* is extinction (other than extinction of *tanha*, extinction of self), but rather that it is an absorption into the universal, into a manifestation of energy beyond rebirth and beyond extinction.

Edward Conze in *Buddhism: Its Essence and Development* puts it this way: "We are told (by Buddhists) that *nirvana* is permanent, stable, imperishable, immovable, ageless, deathless, unborn, and unbecome, that it is power, bliss and happiness, the secure refuge, the shelter, the place of unassailable safety; that it is the real *Truth* and the supreme *Reality*; that it is the *Good*, the supreme goal and the one and only consummation of our life, the eternal, hidden and incomprehensible Peace."

When a Buddhist monk is ordained his family and friends wish him success in following the path to *nirvana*. For him it is a rigorous and demanding path, too rigorous and too demanding for the layperson. The question often arises, is *nirvana* attainable only by the monk and not by the layperson? The contemporary Buddhist teaching is that *nirvana* is attainable by the layperson.

Phra Santi, like other contemporary monks, offers the lay Buddhist the comfort and hope of attaining enlightenment. And is enlightenment not, after all, he says, *nirvana*? I wonder about this, although I am not deterred from following the path despite my feeling that true *nirvana* is for the monk only. Close association with Buddhist monks has persuaded me that only they—the devoted monks—merit true *nirvana*. They sacrifice so much for it. They strive so strenuously for it. They devote their every waking hour to it. The lay Buddhist, like me, should, realistically, settle for the other many benefits which the practice affords. And, I believe, most lay Buddhists—Eastern as well as Western—do so compromise.

The Buddha taught that human beings are, as a result of their *karma*, at differing stages of development, of perfection, and of progress on the 'Path'. Those who are least advanced, least developed, have the longest road to travel towards enlightenment; those who are most advanced have the shortest. Buddhism has a lovely analogy likening man in his stages of spiritual development to a lotus: the stalk rises from the mud, ascends through the water, breaks through the surface, blossoms and reaches for the sky. Rare is the individual who 'blossoms'.

It's appropriate at this point to look at the life of the Buddhist monk—"the good life" of the monastic order and those individuals who are closest to "blossoming".

SIX: THE BUDDHIST MONK

Since a Buddhist monk is not required to make a lifetime commitment, there are those who wear the robes for only a brief period of time—a few weeks, a few months, even a few days—as well as those who remain in the monkhood for many years or for a lifetime.

In Theravadan Buddhist countries like Thailand, which I know best, a man is regarded as "unfinished" if he has not served, for however briefly, as a monk. Therefore, most young men will be ordained, usually before marriage, for a period of three months, during the rainy season lasting from mid-July to mid-October. This period is called *Khao Pansa* and is sometimes referred to as the Buddhist Lent, although it is in no way analogous to the Christian Lent, and, traditionally, it has become a time when Buddhist laymen undertake their short-term ordinations.

One of the motives for a short-term ordination is to 'earn merit' for one's parents—and a strong motive it is. Another is to prepare oneself for life as a layman, householder, and family head.

While in robes, the short-term monk lives under the same conditions and with the same disciplines as the long-term monk. Each morning he leaves the temple grounds to make his neighborhood rounds carrying his alms bowl, in which local residents place food for his sustenance. He eats only two meals during the day—some eat only one meal—and after noon no food, except liquids, is eaten. He meditates, he chants, he studies the *Dhamma*, (Buddhist teachings), he obeys all the monastic precepts. Yet he is best perceived as a layman wearing the robes temporarily, rather than as a monk who has renounced the layman life. (A monk may disrobe whenever he wishes, with the permission of his abbot, permission which is never denied and easily granted.)

It is the renunciate monk who concerns us in what follows, the monk who has dedicated himself to following the path. Such monks fall into two categories, those who dwell in a monastic community in temple grounds and those who dwell in a solitary, hermitic state removed from monastic or lay society, the 'forest monk'. Both categories of monks devote themselves to the pursuit of enlightenment, of *nirvana*, the forest monk to the virtual exclusion of all other activities, the temple monk occasionally involved in lay community affairs, such as participating in Buddhist holy-day or ground-breaking ceremonies, in consecration of new homes or businesses, in funeral and cremation rites, and so on, and frequently involved in teaching novice monks, short-term monks, laymen and laywomen, either in formal groups or individually.

The renunciate monk is a man of extraordinary character and virtue. He has detached himself from family, from career, from all secular affairs, from the pursuit of money, even the retention of money. He is chaste, he is poor, he has few possessions: his robes, his alms bowl, his needle and thread, his water strainer. He is a mendicant, dependent almost totally on the beneficence of the lay community, which regards the giving of alms to monks as a privileged opportunity to earn merit.

A temple monk lives in a simple *khuti*, a spartanly furnished hut with a low, narrow bed, hard mattress, straight-backed chair, perhaps a simple table, perhaps shelving on the walls for his books and texts. A forest monk lives under a special kind of umbrella-tent, sleeps on a mat, and has no material comforts whatsoever.

When a monk goes on his rounds he accepts whatever foods are placed in his alms bowl. He never asks for anything, accepting what is offered, standing silently, with eyes lowered, until after the offering is made, when he may chant a brief blessing for the donor.

When a layperson visits a monk to socialize, or to ask for advice on a problem, or to discuss Buddhism he or she will usually bring fruits, flowers, delicacies, or such necessities as medical supplies and toiletries, and sometimes cash for personal needs. Some laypersons 'sponsor' a monk and undertake to provide his needs. Laypersons will often invite monks to their homes for a pre-noon meal.

Monks rise at an early hour, when the temple gongs are sounded. After attending to their personal toilet, dressing, washing, grooming, and their household cleaning, they meditate until it is "light enough to see clearly the palm of your hand" and then they make their alms rounds, after which they return to their quarters for their morning meal. Many monks settle for just one morning meal; some will have a second meal, starting shortly after 11 a.m. so that it may be completed before noon. The rest of the day is devoted to meditation, reading, studying, perhaps an afternoon nap, and attendance at twilight ceremonial chantings. At night the monk retires for six hours, sometimes only four hours, of sleep. His is an austere, ascetic life, in which he has renounced the secular world for the opportunity of a life of contemplation and pursuit of the path. He shaves his hair (and in Thailand also his eyebrows), symbolic of his rejection of ego and vanity.

Serenity, gentility, and compassion characterize the renunciate monk. He constantly trains himself to detach from anger, to detach from greed, to detach from delusion.

He cultivates ethical conduct to a degree seldom attained by laypersons. He regards as practical, meaningful, and mandatory the Buddha's advice for leading the good life.

He cultivates mental discipline. Unlike the layperson who may devote twenty minutes daily to meditation, the monk devotes most of his waking hours to the practice of both *Samatha* and

Vipassana. Meditation is, after all, the essential element of his monasterial seclusion.

He cultivates insight-wisdom: knowledge of *dukkha*, rejection of egoistic desire, and especially detachment from 'self'. He fights—the Buddha called him a "warrior"—against defilements and for enlightenment. His path to *nirvana* is unwavering, every hour of his day, every day of his monkhood.

Needless to say, the monk deserves to be, and is, admired, respected, and revered by all Buddhist laypersons. The young monk who may wear the robes for only a few weeks or months is honored by his peers in proportion to his time of service. The renunciate monk is honored without reservation. In Thailand, even His Majesty the King (who himself was ordained as a temporary monk), pays obeisance to the monks.

The Buddhist monkhood, known as the *Sangha*, welcomes Westerners, quite a few of whom have come to Buddhist countries to be ordained and to live on temple grounds. Phra Santi, himself a Westerner, sees in this a new and inspiring source for Buddhism. Western monks he has known (and instructed, and sponsored for ordination) are, he believes, singularly sincere, dedicated, and devoted to spiritual cultivation, sometimes even more so than Asians who turn temporarily to the monkhood. A Westerner who decides to wear the robes, even temporarily, Phra Santi believes, has given it much thought, is strongly and properly motivated, and is therefore properly prepared to undergo the material deprivations of monkhood in order to enjoy the spiritual nourishments and rewards. In turn, his ordination strengthens Buddhism and the monastic order.

Women are precluded from full Buddhist monastic participation. They cannot be monks, primarily because their presence in a monastic community would be potentially distracting to males who have taken a vow of chastity. However, they may, in somewhat limited ways, participate in monastic communities, and they are, like people of any race, color, creed, sex or social status, most enthusiastically encouraged to follow the path. Female monastic participation involves the donning of white robes, shaving the head and eyebrows (similar to monks), and living in compounds set aside for *mae-chees*, Buddhist nuns. The Buddhist nun has little in common with the Christian nun, except insofar as they both seek spiritual fulfillment. And, even without taking the limited vows and precepts of the *mae-chee*, women may come to a temple compound and live there for a time as lay practitioners, meditating, reading, and studying under monk teachers.

(Phra Santi believes that in these changing times the role of women in the Buddhist community may soon be considerably enlarged, and the restrictions on female participation considerably liberalized. Even so, he believes, that there is no reason why women, even the most 'liberated', should feel they are discriminated against, or restrained from following the path. Successful practice of the Noble Eightfold Path, he says, has nothing to do with gender and depends only on the perfections we cultivate.)

Those who wear the robes, as monks or as *mae-chees* are relatively few in number. Most Buddhists, Western or Asian, are laypersons. For them, following the path is spiritually nourishing, morally gratifying, and mentally rewarding. It can lead to enlightenment. It may lead, though the path is so different from that of the renunciate monk, to *nirvana*. Even if it falls short of that ultimate goal, it can, and does, lead to "the good life".

SEVEN: THE GOOD LIFE FOR THE LAYPERSON

When one considers that the Buddha's discourses on the good life for the layperson were delivered some two thousand five hundred years ago one can only marvel at their relevance today. They are derived from his teachings on morality, and they cover virtually every aspect of everyday life. Though some today may regard them as homiletic and idealistic, those who follow the path try as best they can to behave as the Buddha recommended, remembering that the Buddha never commanded, "you must"; instead he said, "try".

What the Buddha said is transcribed below for the most part in his words, as translated in various books of the Pali canon, and modified only in some instances by me for better contemporary comprehension.

ON FAMILY BEHAVIOR

In a loving family the home will be like a flower garden. Family discord is like a storm that plays havoc with the garden. When family discord arises do not blame others, but rather examine your own motives, attitudes, and behavior. Even a small misunderstanding, if allowed to develop into serious discord, can bring on family misfortune and disaster. Guard against even the smallest misunderstandings in family life.

ON CHILDREN AND PARENTS

Children should be attentive to their parent's needs. They should not squander their parents' wealth. They should provide for their parents in their old age. They should perform the funeral rites for their parents.

Parents should discipline their children which means teaching and training them to avoid bad behavior. They should provide their children with good education. They should see to it that they marry into good families. They should pass on their assets to their children.

Heads of families should build economic security through acquiring sufficient wealth by just and righteous means. They should spend liberally but prudently on behalf of themselves, their family, their relatives, their friends, and on deeds which accumulate merit. They should remain free from debt.

ON HUSBANDS AND WIVES

Husbands should accord their wives courtesy, respect, and honor (wives should reciprocate). They should be loving and faithful. They should give their wives authority. They should make life secure and comfortable for their wives. They should make their wives happy by giving them clothing and jewelry.

Wives should manage the household. They should be hospitable and gracious to guests, friends, relatives, and husbands' employees. They should be loving and faithful. They should be thrifty and non-profligate with their husband's earnings. They should be alert, intelligent, and efficient.

(There is little here to upset today's liberated woman, except perhaps manage the household. The Buddha might have amended that had he been able to forecast the contemporary status of women.)

ON FRIENDS, RELATIVES, AND NEIGHBORS

They should behave with hospitality and generosity toward one other. They should speak gently and cordially. They should see to one another's welfare. They should not be quarrelsome or disputatious. They should offer a helping hand in times of need. They should not abandon those in difficult straits.

ON FALSE FRIENDS AND TRUE FRIENDS

A false friend is one who exploits you financially, who takes from you and does not give in return, who is selfish, who is overly complimentary, who flatters excessively, who agrees with whatever you say or do, who praises you to your face and slanders you behind your back, who makes excuses when asked to do you a favor.

A true friend is one who gives you sound advice, who is sympathetic, who is steadfast, who protects you when you need defense, protects your property when you are negligent, shelters you in times of distress, helps in every way possible to increase your fortune, who confides in you and in whom you may confide, who discourages your vices and encourages your virtues, who shares your sorrows, rejoices in your joys, rebukes those who speak ill of you, commends those who speak well of you, who would make the ultimate sacrifice if needed to save your life.

ON EMPLOYERS AND EMPLOYEES

Employers should assign to their employees only tasks which their employees have the physical strength and the mental capability of handling. They should pay adequate wages and should provide for medical needs. They should give their employees vacations and bonuses.

Employees should work energetically and not shirk their responsibilities. They should be honest and never cheat their employers. They should be forthright and attentive. They should speak well of their employers.

(The Buddha's time was one of masters and servants. And this is still true in countries like Thailand where households, even of modest means, employ servants. One of the Buddha's admonitions to employee-servants was: arise before your masters do, retire after they do. This was regarded—still is in Thailand—as not being exploitative but rather as contributing to the orderliness and well-being of the household.)

The Buddha said further: Those who cheat in business, those who swindle or deceive, hurt themselves as well as those whom they cheat, for the deeds and misdeeds of people (*karma*) remain within themselves.

And he gave this additional advice for the business person: one-fourth of your income should be spent on current needs, one-fourth should be saved for future needs, two-fourths should be reinvested in your business.

ON MALE BEHAVIOR TOWARD A FEMALE

A male should speak to a female with a pure heart. If she is old he should regard her as lovingly as he would his mother. If she is older than he, he should regard her as respectfully as he would an older sister. If she is younger than he, he should regard her as considerately as he would a younger sister. If she is a child he should treat her deferentially and politely.

ON SOCIAL BEHAVIOR

Abstain from backbiting and slander, from language that may cause hatred, enmity, disunity, disharmony. Abstain from language that is harsh, rude, impolite, malicious, abusive. Abstain from idle, foolish babble. Abstain from gossip. If you cannot say anything friendly, benevolent, meaningful, and useful, keep a noble silence.

Be tolerant with the intolerant. Be mild with the violent. If you have power over others be gentle, especially with the weak. Be patient, restrained, compassionate.

Be free from greed among the greedy. Do not seek to gain by the loss of others.

Instead of finding fault in others, look to your own misdeeds. Do not judge harshly. See both sides, and judge fairly.

Do not deceive nor despise nor wish harm to another person. Meet hatred with kindness, evil with goodness, greed with generosity, lies with truth.

A person's position in society is not determined by birth, but by worth, not by descent but by conduct and character. Try to treat all people alike. You will understand others insofar as you understand yourself. You will sympathize with others when you realize that they experience the same suffering (*dukkha*) as you. Love others as you love yourself. Protecting yourself through mindfulness you protect others; protecting others through kindness and patience you protect yourself.

ON RELIGIONS

Do not decry, depreciate, or condemn the religions of others. Honor whatever in them is worthy of honor. Listen, be curious, be willing to understand the doctrines of others.

ON BENEFICIAL ACTIVITIES

These things, the Buddha taught, benefit all persons:

In your job, trade, craft, or profession be skilled, efficient, earnest, energetic, knowledgeable. Protect your income. Spend in proportion to your income, not too much, not too little. Do not be avaricious. Do not hoard wealth. Do not be extravagant, but live within your means.

Associate with good friends who are faithful, learned, virtuous, liberal, intelligent and those who will help you along the right path and away from evil.

Have faith and confidence in moral, spiritual, and intellectual values.

Practice charity and generosity without attachment to wealth or craving for wealth.

ON WEALTH

There are four requirements for accumulating wealth: determined energy, conservation of what is earned, living simply, associating with good people.

When you have accumulated wealth, do not consider it as wholly your own. Share with others. Set aside some for the needs of your community and your nation. Set aside some for the needs of religious teachers. Save some for emergencies.

And always remember that the greatest wealth is contentedness.

ON CHARITY AND GENEROSITY

Cultivate wholesomeness by giving useful things to those who are in need: food, clothing, money. Be charitable even if you are poor, but not to the detriment of your own welfare.

A truly virtuous person helps those in need purely out of compassion, not out of hope for personal gain or the accumulation of merit, and without caring whether one's generosity is seen or acknowledged.

ON UNETHICAL CONDUCT

The Buddha counseled all laypersons to avoid all manifestations of unethical conduct, to wit: hostility and malice toward others, hypocrisy, deceitfulness, stealing the property of others, defrauding creditors by denying that debts are owed them, bearing false witness, adultery, failure to support elderly parents.

He counseled them to avoid offending, by words or blows, any members of the family, giving false advice, failing to return another's hospitality, making others angry.

He urged them to reject avarice, envy, cunning, cruelty, and harsh language.

He bade them to undertake the rules of training in the practice of the Five Precepts.

(1) ON HOSTILITY

Hatred cannot be appeased by hatred. Hatred cannot be appeased by thinking that that person abused me, beat me, defeated me, or robbed me. Do not hate those who hate you. Hatred can only be appeased by love.

Do not speak harshly to others; they will only answer harshly. Angry speech brings trouble. Bear insult without making an angry reply. The just man does not resort to winning by violence.

(2) ON INTEMPERANCE

The dangers of heedless intoxication, the Buddha said, are: squandering of wealth, argumentativeness, risk of illness, risk of scandal, rejection by society, and weakening of the mind.

(3) ON THE SQUANDERING OF WEALTH

The following activities, the Buddha said, lead to the dissipation of wealth: indulging in intoxicants, carousing (literally, "spending the night wandering about the town"), nightclubbing (literally, "haunting fairs"), gambling, keeping bad company, and idleness.

(4) ON IDLENESS

The idle person finds many excuses to avoid working: It is too hot to work. It is too cold. It is too early to work. It is too late. I have not eaten enough to work. I have eaten too much. Such a person goes through life neglecting duty and responsibility, failing to acquire assets, and failing to preserve whatever assets may already have been possessed.

If something is to be done, do it vigorously.

ON CRIMINAL THEFT

The cause is poverty. Punishment of wrong-doers is futile. Improved economic conditions are essential to the eradication of criminal theft.

ON THOSE WHO GOVERN

The Buddha proposed ten rules for those who govern. These rules were addressed to the kings of his time, and they apply today to heads of states, political leaders, legislative, judicial, or executive leaders, to any one who holds public trust and is responsible for the public good:

1. Be liberal, generous, charitable. Do not use your position to accumulate wealth and property.

2. Obey the five precepts: do not destroy life, lie, steal, engage in illicit sex, use intoxicants heedlessly.

3. Make the welfare of your people your paramount concern .

4. Govern with integrity. Do not deceive your people.

5. Be kind, gentle, and genial.

6. Lead a simple life, self-controlled, non-sybaritic.

7. Be free of hatred toward anybody.

8. Promote peace and non-violence.

9. Be patient, tolerant, forbearing.

10. Do not oppose the will of the people.

ON SOURCES OF HAPPINESS

In concluding this section on the good life for the layperson, here is what the Buddha prescribed in his *Mahamangala Sutta* as the ten sources of happiness for the layperson:

1. To serve the wise and to honor those who deserve honor.

2. To dwell in a pleasant land, to have done good works in a former birth, to nurture right desires.

3. To cultivate clarity of mind, a pleasant manner of speech, learning, self-mastery.

4. To support one's parents, to cherish one's spouse and children, to follow a peaceful calling.

5. To give alms, to live with uprightness, to help one's kin, to act beyond reproach.

6. To abhor and cease from evil, to abstain from intoxicants, to persist in well-doing.

7. To be reverent and humble, to be content and grateful, to study the *Dhamma* (the Buddhist teachings).

8. To be patient and gentle, to keep the company of peaceful, non-violent persons, to speak properly of spiritual matters.

9. To be self-restrained, to know the Four Noble Truths, to realize *nirvana*.

10. To develop equanimity, to avoid yielding to grief or to passion.

A BUDDHIST'S CREED

I will conduct myself with ethical rectitude in all my actions, all my thoughts.

I will treat all people, all sentient beings, with sympathetic understanding, with compassion, with loving-kindness.

I will resist anger.

I will desist from greed.

I will cultivate mental tranquility.

I will meditate; I will be aware of all my actions, all my thoughts.

I will reject egoistic desire, all notions of a unity called self, all notions of permanence.

I will not regret the past nor fret about the future.

I will develop equanimity; I will not allow myself to exult in my good fortune or to despair in my bad fortune.

I will strive to the best of my ability for enlightenment.

GENERAL GLOSSARY

anatta The concept of 'no-self'—there is no absolute soul or self; one of the three characteristics of existence.

anicca Impermanence; one of the three characteristics of existence.

bo tree A fig tree under which the Buddha attained enlightenment.

Bodghaya The town in northern India where the Buddha attained enlightenment.

Buddha 'The Enlightened One' as Siddartha Gotama became known after he reached nirvana under the Bo tree.

dhamma The teachings of Buddhism.

dukkha The suffering of life on earth which is meant to be transcended by following the Buddhist Path.

jhanas Trance-like states of concentration

karma The Buddhist concept of cause and effect that transcends individual lifetimes.

Kasina A type of meditation where one concentrates on a colored disc and then recalls the image as a means of developing calm and concentration to quiet the mind.

khandas The five aggregates that make up the human being: body, feelings, perceptions, predispositions, and consciousness.

Khao Pansa The three month long 'Buddhist Lent' in Thailand at the beginning of the rainy season when many boys enter the monkood.

khuti The modest living quaters of a monk (as called in Thailand)

mae-chee A Buddhist nun as they are called in Thailand.

Mahamangala Sutta A sutta in which the Buddha describes the ten sources of happiness for the layperson.

Mahayana Buddhism The form of Buddhism practiced in Tibet, China, Japan, Mongolia and Korea. Also known as 'the greater vehicle'.

metta Universal love

nirvana The ultimate goal of Buddhist practice: enlightenment.

'om mani padme hum' The best known Buddhist mantra, or chant, used during and for meditation. See text for a complete translation of its meaning.

Pali The ancient religious language of India in which the Theravadan Buddhist teachings were first written down. Sanskrit did the same for the Mahayana Buddhist teachings.

parinirvana The death of Buddha

Samatha A type of meditation where one tries to ignore all sensory diversions. The exact opposite of 'Vipassana meditation'.

Sangha The organized body of practicing monks are known as the 'Sangha'.

Siddartha Gotama The Buddhas birthright name.

sukkha The antithesis of 'dukkha', sukkha describes the existence of happiness, joy, achievement, fulfillment and well-being.

suttas (or sutras) The Buddhist discourses, called 'sutras' in Sanskrit.

tanha Craving, desire and attachment—the major hurdles to be overcome in order to reach enlightenment or become an ethical and moral person.

tankha A Tibetan religious painting scroll which depicts the Buddhist cosmology.

Tantrayana Buddhism (See Vajrayana Buddhism)

tantric Esoteric Buddhist practices based upon oral transmission rather than written text.

Taoism An ancient Chinese philosophy based upon the principles of nature and the inter-play of opposite forces.

The Five Aggregates The five aggregates, known as the five *khandas*, that make up the human being: body, feelings, perceptions, predispositions, and consciousness.

The Five Precepts The Buddhist code of moral behavior—see text for complete outline.

The Four Noble Truths The teachings of Buddha are based on 'The Four Noble Truths': there is suffering, the cause of suffering is egoistic desire, the elimination of egoistic desire eliminates suffering, the way to the elimination of egoistic desire is by following The Noble Eightfold Path.

The Four Passing Sights The sights that Siddartha Gotama encountered when he first left the confines of his palace and which impressed upon him the transitory nature of life.

The Noble Eightfold Path The eight steps towards enlightenment along the path of Buddhist practice and towards the elimination of suffering.

The Triple Gems The Buddha, the Sangha (monastic community), and the Dhamma (the teachings of Buddhism)

Theravada Buddhism The form of Buddhism practiced in Thailand, Burma, Laos, Cambodia, Sri Lanka, and Nepal. Also known as Hinayana ('the lesser vehicle') and 'The Way of the Elders'.

Vajrayana Buddhism An esoteric form of Mahayana Buddhism practised in Tibet and also known as the 'Diamond Vehicle'.

Vippassana A type of meditation that cultivates mental awareness of the physical world around us. The opposite of 'Samatha meditation'.

Way of the Elders The name which Theravadans call their form of Buddhism. Theravada Buddhism is also sometimes called 'the old wisdom school' since the scriptures are derived from the teachings of the Buddha as recorded in the earliest written texts.

Zen Buddhism A permutation of Mahayana Buddhism as practiced by some in Japan.